BE THE Change! POLITICAL PARTICIPATION IN YOUR COMMUNITY™

DEVELOPING POLITICAL LEADERSHIP SKILLS

Tiffanie Drayton

Rosen YA
New York

Published in 2020 by The Rosen Publishing Group, Inc.
29 East 21st Street, New York, NY 10010

Copyright © 2020 by The Rosen Publishing Group, Inc.

First Edition

All rights reserved. No part of this book may be reproduced in any form without permission in writing from the publisher, except by a reviewer.

Library of Congress Cataloging-in-Publication Data

Names: Drayton, Tiffanie, author.
Title: Developing political leadership skills / Tiffanie Drayton.
Description: New York : Rosen Publishing, 2020 | Series: Be the change! political participation in your community | Includes bibliographical references and index. | Audience: Grade 7 to 12.
Identifiers: LCCN 2019009962| ISBN 9781725340787 (library bound) | ISBN 9781725340770 (pbk.)
Subjects: LCSH: Political participation—United States—Juvenile literature. | Political leadership—United States—Juvenile literature. | Political candidates—United States—Juvenile literature. | Political activists—United States—Juvenile literature.
Classification: LCC JK1764 .D73 2019 | DDC 303.3/4—dc23
LC record available at https://lccn.loc.gov/2019009962

Manufactured in the United States of America

CONTENTS

INTRODUCTION **4**

CHAPTER ONE
**WHAT DOES IT TAKE TO
BE A POLITICAL LEADER?** **7**

CHAPTER TWO
**INSPIRING AND CULTIVATING
THE LEADER IN YOU** **20**

CHAPTER THREE
THE SKILLS OF A POLITICAL LEADER **32**

CHAPTER FOUR
GET TRAINED, GET INVOLVED!........... **42**

GLOSSARY **53**
FOR MORE INFORMATION............. **55**
FOR FURTHER READING................ **58**
BIBLIOGRAPHY....................... **59**
INDEX............................... **61**

INTRODUCTION

Most stories about great leaders focus on the remarkable impact they had on the world. Sojourner Truth escaped from slavery to become one of the most influential speakers on civil rights and abolition. Abraham Lincoln courageously took a stand against slavery and steered the United States through the trauma of the Civil War, ultimately ending slavery and forcing the country to stand on the right side of history. Barack Obama became the first black president of the United States after serving as an Illinois state senator and working as a grassroots community organizer in Chicago. But what is often left out of these remarkable stories is how these great women and men developed the key skills they needed to become inspiring leaders and make a change.

The truth is that leaders are made, not born. Everyone is born with the capacity to become a great leader, but not everyone gets the opportunity to develop his or her natural-born talents. This is especially true for those who have limited access to political education and economic resources. Although there are millions of young people in America, the voices of youth are among the most excluded in politics. Young people often struggle to gain the respect of older politicians, who may view them as uninformed and lacking necessary leadership skills. As

INTRODUCTION 5

Sojourner Truth was born into slavery and escaped to become a prominent activist in the civil rights movement. She was a skilled and inspiring leader.

Developing Political Leadership Skills

a result, they are left out of political conversations and not allowed to take part in decision making, even when they will be directly affected by the outcomes.

Young people who are interested in making their voices heard in the political arena can take a stand to change this situation. By understanding what it means to be a political leader, developing leadership skills, and becoming more aware of political issues, young people can break down the barriers to their political involvement and demand to be heard. Whether it be by running for student council to ensure schools hear and respond to the needs of their student body, starting a campaign to raise awareness about a particular issue, or working toward a bigger goal, such as running for office or even becoming the president of the United States, there are many ways that savvy aspiring leaders can sharpen their skills, participate in the political process, and have a real impact in their own communities and beyond. As Harriet Tubman once said, "Every great dream begins with a dreamer. Always remember, you have within you the strength, the patience, and the passion to reach for the stars to change the world."

CHAPTER ONE

WHAT DOES IT TAKE TO BE A POLITICAL LEADER?

There are many different kinds of political leaders and many different ways a person can become one. Some people become political leaders by running for office in the local, state, or federal government. Others are thrust into the role after taking a stand for something that they believe in. The two most common types of political leaders are elected officials and political activists. Each has unique roles and expectations, but they ultimately share an important

There are many ways to serve as a leader. One of those ways is to be elected to your local school board.

duty: to advocate for and protect the populations they represent.

WHAT ARE ELECTED OFFICIALS?

An elected official, or politician, is a person who is elected to political office. There are many kinds of elected officials who serve the public with varying degrees of power and influence. Local elected officials operate within a small jurisdiction (a school, city, town, or neighborhood) and represent the people in their immediate community. For example, residents in school districts typically elect their school board members, who are responsible for implementing local school policies and budgeting, overseeing the employment of superintendents, and ensuring school facilities are properly cared for. Other examples of local politicians include city council members, county commissioners, and mayors. These local elected officials have similar roles and responsibilities. They represent their constituencies, enact legislation and policy, and oversee budgeting. The main difference between these positions is their sphere of influence. School board members are appointed to manage local schools, while the

What Does It Take to Be a Political Leader?

mayor of a town presides over all other members of the local government to make sure an entire town or city is run with the needs of its community in mind.

When it comes to national politics, the first position that most people think of is usually the president, and

Members are sworn in to the House of Representatives' 116th Congress on Capitol Hill on January 3, 2019, in Washington, DC.

with good reason. The president holds the highest level of political office and is responsible for running the entire country. However, contrary to popular belief, the president doesn't have limitless power. Congress, comprised of senators and members of the House of Representatives, is made up of hundreds of political leaders who are responsible for everything from voting to pass legislation to even potentially impeaching the president if necessary. There are many different kinds of political leaders, all with distinct and important roles.

EVERYTHING YOU NEED TO KNOW ABOUT RUNNING FOR OFFICE

Running for office in a local, state, or federal election comes with many responsibilities. Upon announcing candidacy, political candidates' lives become about their constituent base—whom they will represent if they win the election. That may be just a few hundred or thousand people, for example, if they are running for a position on a school board or city council. In a large state or US congressional district, a political leader will represent thousands or even millions of people. As international leaders, presidents represent not only their country, but should also serve the interests of the billions of people worldwide. There are many ways that candidates strive to demonstrate to the public that they have the skills, education, and ability to meet these expectations.

MIKE FLOYD: ONE OF AMERICA'S YOUNGEST SCHOOL BOARD MEMBERS

As a high school senior in Pearland, Texas, Mike Floyd ran for school board against opponents who had the support of his district's member of Congress and state representative. No one expected he could beat them. However, Floyd had long been committed to student organizing, and that commitment gave him an unlikely advantage. In the fourth grade, he started a petition to change the district's food service contract that received four hundred signatures and led to negotiations for a new contract. As a junior in high school, he worked with his peers to get six thousand signatures on a petition to challenge his school's use of in-school suspension for minor infractions. Floyd understood the power and importance of students—a demographic his competitors overlooked. By tapping into student networks, he won a seat on the Pearland ISD School Board, becoming one of the youngest people in the United States ever to sit on a school board.

MAINTAINING A GOOD PUBLIC IMAGE

Political candidates must know how to manage the public's perception of them. One of the longest-standing political customs in the United States is for politicians to be photographed kissing babies. While this may seem frivolous (and a great way to spread germs!), it is a great example of how political candidates manage their public image. Though the origins of political baby kissing is unclear, President Andrew Jackson is credited with being the first to use a baby as a prop while touring the United States in 1833. While on tour, Jackson, then known for being kind to all people, was approached by a poor woman holding a boy with a dirty face. According to the University of Michigan's *Cosmopolitan* magazine, published in 1887, Jackson reached out for the boy and exclaimed, "Ah! There is a fine specimen of American childhood. I think, madam, your boy will make a fine man someday." Then, he put the dirty face of the infant close to the face of his secretary of war, General Eaton, saying, "Eaton, kiss him?" While the crowd laughed, General Eaton pretended to lay a wet one on the child and then Jackson handed the baby back to the happy mother.

Before long, political candidates started kissing babies themselves. The kissing served two purposes: to win the support of parents and to promote a loving, fatherly image. Just about every president has been captured in a photo kissing a baby at some point.

Kissing babies is not the only way a political candidate can project a wholesome public image. Candidates are expected to maintain their appearance, keeping themselves properly groomed and dressing professionally. A political candidate should also attend as many meetings, events, and community celebrations as possible to ensure that their constituents know their face and name. Depending on how high profile the

What Does It Take to Be a Political Leader? 13

political race is, candidates may be publicly scrutinized by the press. The personal lives of candidates are not off limits to this scrutiny and should reflect the values and opinions they publicly express. The easiest way for a candidate to lose the trust of the public is by lacking honesty and integrity.

Former president Barack Obama kissing a baby in true presidential fashion. Kissing babies has become a tradition for presidents and presidential candidates.

PARTICIPATING IN DEBATES AND FORUMS

Public debates and forums provide a way for political candidates to express their positions on various issues in hopes of winning the support and votes of their constituency. Political candidates should be able to express deep interest and knowledge of the issues that matter to voters, as well as be ready to defend their positions. Debates and forums give political candidates the opportunity to face off with other candidates and put their verbal and intellectual prowess on full display. When participating in a debate or forum, it is important that candidates come prepared and deliver clear speeches that stay on theme and have a simple but powerful message.

WHAT ARE POLITICAL ACTIVISTS?

Malala Yousafzai was only fifteen years old when she made a public speech about girls' right to learn. In her country of birth, Pakistan, girls were barred from receiving an education by the Taliban—an extreme political organization that took control of parts of the country. The region where Malala and her family lived was one of those areas controlled by the Taliban. Malala believed this practice of restricting girls' education to be both cruel and unfair, so she took a stand for girls' rights and almost paid for that decision with her life. One day after her speech, a masked

MARCH FOR OUR LIVES: THE STUDENT-LED PROTEST ORGANIZED WITH THE HELP OF TECHNOLOGY

On February 14, 2018, the lives of students at Marjory Stoneman Douglas High School were changed forever when a gunman opened fire and killed seventeen students and faculty members. Four days later, Cameron Kasky, a junior at the school, and some of his classmates took action. They announced plans for a demonstration in Washington, DC, to urge the government to implement stronger gun laws. At least two million people participated in the March for Our Lives demonstration and its over eight hundred sister marches across the country, according to Ryan Sit in *Newsweek*. The march has been celebrated as among the biggest youth-led movements in American history, and technology had everything to do with its success.

The students looked to Brady Kriss, founder of Ragtag, an organization that connects tech expert volunteers with political activists, for help. Within a day, a full team of experts was working hard to help the teens organize, mobilize, and fundraise. The organization created and managed a website with important information and links to ally movements, as well as a page to collect donations. It also launched a texting operation to help with outreach. With the help of Ragtag, the students were able to organize their march quickly and capitalize on the momentum of the moment.

man boarded her school bus and asked, "Who is Malala?" The gunman shot her on the left side of her head, intending to kill her. Ten days later, she awoke in a hospital in England and her life would never be the same.

Her story sparked an international conversation about the inequality girls and women face under the rule of the Taliban, and she became the face of a movement to give girls access to education. Within a few years, Malala became one of the most prominent young political activists of her generation. In 2014, she became the youngest person ever to win a Nobel Peace Prize.

Like Malala, political activists challenge the law and the status quo. Some famous American activists include civil rights leaders Martin Luther King Jr. and Rosa Parks, feminist activist Gloria Steinem, and transgender rights activist Jazz Jennings. Public appearances, speeches, demonstrations, strikes, marches, and sit-ins are all common ways that activists work to bring about the change they want to see in the world.

With the advent of new technologies, activists are finding other new, revolutionary ways to make their voices heard. Social media has inspired a whole new form of activism, referred to by many as hashtag activism. One well-known example is the Black Lives Matter movement, one of the first social media driven movements, which was started to increase awareness of police brutality and racism. The hashtag #BlackLivesMatter began to be used in 2013 after the acquittal of George Zimmerman in the shooting death of Trayvon Martin, a black teenager, in February 2012. Other popular political hashtags include #MeToo (a movement started by Tarana Burke against sexual harassment and sexual assault) and Donald Trump's political rallying cry #MAGA (Make America

What Does It Take to Be a Political Leader?

Malala Yousafzai waves after delivering a speech to students in Mexico. Yousafzai is a Pakastani Nobel Prize laureate known for her education advocacy for girls and women.

Great Again). Though the effectiveness of hashtag movements is often debated, there's no doubt that social media is an important tool for political activists to raise awareness about their causes.

POLITICAL ACTIVISM AND TECHNOLOGY

For many political activists who have identified a cause or a problem, technology can help them come up with solutions. Sixto Cancel grew up in foster care and understood the unique experiences and difficulties of young people raised in that system. In high school, he launched Stellar Works, a program that offered after-school tutoring and transportation for students with a history of being involved in foster care. He also founded and launched Think of Us, a life coaching web and mobile application, to provide foster care youth with extended support. The app empowers youth by helping them to build a stronger support system and also focus on personal advancement.

Cancel is one of many young people who decided to use technology to address important real-world issues. The ways political activists can use technology to create solutions and drive change are endless.
For example, after hearing about the Flint, Michigan, water crisis, thirteen-year-old Gitanjali Rao wanted to help and turned to technology to do so. In a matter of months, she developed a portable device that could quickly detect the levels of lead in water at a fraction of the cost of what was already on the market. This device delivers the information directly to a user's cellphone.

Tired of witnessing the devastation of wildfires, Aditya Shah and Sanjana Shah, two teens living in California, created the Smart Wildfire Sensor, a device that uses weather data and measurements of flammable matter in the sky to predict the likelihood of a fire. The teens hope the device will be able to protect homes, save lives, and lower firefighting costs across the scorched region.

All these teens demonstrate that passion can help people to change the world. But first you need to understand yourself and hone your leadership skills.

CHAPTER TWO

INSPIRING AND CULTIVATING THE LEADER IN YOU

What are the common character traits of political leaders? How does a leader develop a leadership style? What drives a leader to do great things? These are all important questions to consider for anyone with aspirations to be a leader.

The ancient Greek philosopher Aristotle once said that "Knowing yourself is the beginning of all wisdom." Every person is unique, born with an individual personality and driven through life by personal passion.

Some people assume that leaders have to be extroverted and outgoing, but that is not true. People with all different personality types can make excellent leaders.

Understanding who you are and what you are passionate about is the key to becoming a great political leader and unlocking your full potential to motivate, connect with, and move others. It also helps you build on your individual strengths and address any weaknesses that could possibly become a barrier to success.

PERSONALITY AND LEADERSHIP

Psychologists believe that people's personalities are made up of traits—patterns of behavior and thought and emotions—that change very little over time. There are many different traits, but three major ones impact a person's ability to be a leader: introversion/extroversion, neuroticism (the tendency to get stressed), and conscientiousness (how careful and diligent a person is). These traits present themselves in different ways from person to person and impact not only a person's leadership style but also a leader's overall effectiveness.

You don't have to be an extrovert to be a great leader. Introverts have many skills that qualify them to connect with people and lead successfully.

INTROVERSION VERSUS EXTROVERSION

Do you always find yourself at the center of the party or do you much prefer a quiet night alone with a great book or movie? After spending a long day out with friends and family, do you need some time alone or are you immediately ready to socialize even more? Many people mistakenly think of extroversion as simply outgoingness and believe that introversion is just another word for being shy, but there is more to the story. An introvert may well seem like the funniest and most outgoing person among a group of friends, but after some time, this person will need personal space to recharge. Extroverts, on the other hand, recharge by socializing even more! It is also important to understand that these two traits exist on a spectrum. Very few people are 100 percent extroverted or introverted, and most people fall somewhere in between the two, just closer to one end of the spectrum than the other.

Both introverts and extroverts have strengths and weaknesses that can impact their ability to be great leaders. While extroverts are often very charismatic, finding it easy to connect with others by sharing feelings and being open, and can be great at collaborating in groups, they often struggle with boredom and find it hard to work alone. They also tend to monopolize conversations and not let others offer ideas or insights. Introverts can sometimes feel like they have gotten the short end of the stick—often left out of the spotlight, feeling withdrawn and disconnected—but introverts are often very insightful, empathetic, self-motivated, and great team

Aspiring leaders can hone their public speaking skills by joining a school club or society where they have the opportunity to speak in front of peers.

players who won't hog the stage. Introverts may not necessarily jump at the opportunity to be in a leadership position, but once given the chance, they may well shine in the role.

TIPS FOR INTROVERTED AND EXTROVERTED LEADERS

The following tips for introverts and extroverts can help you make the most of your personality traits to enhance your leadership skills.

Introverts:
- Spend time reaching out to and connecting with others.
- Prepare what you would like to say in meetings beforehand.
- Communicate one-on-one as often as possible.
- Establish modes of communication other than those involving talking (text, email, social media).

Extroverts:
- Aim to be in a collaborative environment.
- Listen closely to others and appreciate their ideas.
- Ask more questions and invite others to contribute.
- Be careful not to overshare.

NEUROTICISM

Do you become very anxious, racked with fear and self-doubt before a class presentation? Or are you always cool, calm, and collected in the face of a challenge? Are you less likely than your friends to take big risks, overly focused on the possibility of a bad outcome? Neuroticism is a personality trait that exists on a spectrum. On one end of the spectrum is perfect emotional stability and on the other is emotional chaos—the difference between the *Star Wars* robot R2-D2 and the Incredible Hulk. Most people are neither robot nor mad scientist turned green monster and fall somewhere in between these two extremes, but often closer to one end of the spectrum than the

FAMOUS INTROVERTED PRESIDENTS

Introverts are less likely to be in positions of political leadership, but that does not mean they are not fit for the job. There are many historical and present-day introverted political leaders who used their introversion to their advantage and led the United States through trying times. Some of the most notable include American presidents Abraham Lincoln, Thomas Jefferson, John F. Kennedy, Richard Nixon, and Barack Obama. For some, it comes as a surprise that Obama was an introvert because of the way he engaged the public and gave powerful, heartfelt speeches during his presidency, but it is actually the former president's introversion that helped him develop his oratorical skills. Introspection (looking inward), a profound sense of empathy, and a dedication to preparation are just some of the qualities that introverts tend to have, which can make them fantastic public speakers. For that reason, speeches delivered by introverted presidents often top the list of the greatest speeches in history. From Lincoln's Gettysburg Address to Kennedy's inaugural address, speeches by introverted presidents are among the most celebrated.

John F. Kennedy, thirty-fifth president of the United States, was well known for his introverted personality, passionate speeches, and political leadership skills.

other. For young people striving to become leaders, high neuroticism can be a big challenge. Everyone struggles with some degree of neuroticism, but those who experience higher levels of neuroticism are more likely to feel anxious and insecure and lack self-confidence, making it hard to rise to the occasion and be a strong leader. However, just because it is hard does not mean it is impossible. There are many things that can be done to help curb negative feelings and boost confidence.

HOW TO DEAL WITH ANXIETY AND BUILD SELF-CONFIDENCE

There is a big connection between anxiety and low self-confidence. People experience anxiety whenever they think there is a threat or something makes them feel scared. For example, if you have to give a speech in front of your class, you may think that others will laugh at you and this can lead to anxiety. When you are in an anxious state, you lose self-confidence and may be overtaken by self-doubt. Your hands may become sweaty and your speech slurred, increasing the likelihood that your great fear of being made fun of may come true, which will only further erode your self-confidence. It is a vicious cycle. The following tips for managing anxiety and building confidence can help to address these negative thoughts and feelings.

- **Practice deep breathing and meditation.** Learning how to relax is a skill that requires practice, no different from learning how to

Inspiring and Cultivating the Leader in You 27

swing a bat or do a new dance move. Deep breathing and meditation decreases anxiety and it should be practiced daily.
- **Get up, get moving.** Exercise decreases anxiety by releasing many feel-good chemicals in the brain and increasing blood flow. In situations that provoke high anxiety, find a comfortable place to do a few jumping jacks or push-ups. The activity will also help to distract you from anxious thoughts.

Practicing yoga and meditation helps to increase your attention span and improve memory, which are helpful skills for leaders. Effective leaders should know how to practice self-care.

- **Pay attention to the good things.** A great way to keep your mind off the worry track is to focus your thoughts on things that are good, beautiful, and positive. Appreciate the small, everyday blessings. Allow yourself to dream, wish, and imagine the best that could happen.

CONSCIENTIOUSNESS

Is your room currently a mess or is it perfectly organized? Do you like to do things on the spur of moment or do you always like to have a plan? Do your friends think you are very dependable, or do you often flake on plans?

Conscientiousness reflects a person's tendency to be organized, reliable, hardworking, and disciplined. A highly conscientious person is very efficient and organized, whereas a person who is less so tends to be more easygoing and careless. When taken to the extreme, a highly conscientious person can be very inflexible and stubborn. Conversely, those on the opposite end of the spectrum may be very flexible and spontaneous, but unable to commit and follow through with a plan. Though being on either side of the spectrum can present challenges, it has long been documented that conscientious people more often find themselves in leadership positions and tend to be more effective leaders.

Being a political leader is hard work that requires dedication, commitment, and organizational skills that may come more easily to highly conscientious people. Still, people who are naturally conscientious and those who are not can always further develop this important quality by taking steps to be more reliable, organized, and disciplined.

DRIVEN TO ACTION BY CIRCUMSTANCE: DETROIT STUDENTS SUE MICHIGAN FOR THE RIGHT TO AN EDUCATION

Americans have long fought for the fundamental right to an education. However, many students across the nation, especially students of color, are being denied that right. In September 2016, a group of students from the most underperforming schools in Detroit, Michigan, banded together to try to get the government to improve their schools. According to Jacey Fortin in the *New York Times*, their schools were not only infested with rats and roaches, but also suffered because of a lack of funding. As a result, textbooks were outdated, lunches were disgusting, buildings were unsafe and dirty, and worst of all, teachers were failing to educate students. Many students reported that they could not read or were reading well below grade level.

Desperate for change, they decided to sue the state. The lawsuit, *Gary B. v. Snyder*, argued that all students should have the right to literacy because there is no way for people to exercise or understand their constitutional rights, vote, or join the military if they cannot read. However, the courts didn't agree. The lawsuit was dismissed in 2018. Still, this case offers a tool for advocates to fight for education in the courts. It also serves as an example of how people are often driven to action by circumstance and a deep desire to make change.

TIPS FOR INCREASING CONSCIENTIOUSNESS

According to Paul Hammerness and Margaret Moore, authors of *Organize Your Mind, Organize Your Life*, increasing conscientiousness can start with these small steps:

- Set specific goals—like better organizing a room or being more punctual to class—instead of thinking you can change everything all at once. The more specific a goal is, the more likely it will be accomplished.
- Create daily plans and schedules and actually stick to them as best you can! It takes a lot of preparation, focus, and self-discipline not only to make a plan, but also to follow through with one. The more frequently someone practices making plans and sticking to them, the easier it will be to remain focused and on task.
- Watch out for distractions that throw you off course. It is naturally easier for less conscientious people to get distracted, but that is especially true when phones and computers are thrown into the mix. When trying to complete an important task, steer clear of all distractions.

PASSION DRIVES US ALL

Steve Jobs, the cofounder of Apple Inc., once said, "You have to be burning with an idea, or a problem, or a wrong that you want to right. If you're not passionate enough from the start, you'll never stick it out."

Becoming a political leader is a big responsibility. It requires persistence, perseverance, hard work, and dedication. Whether campaigning for a position in student government, launching a campaign to address a community problem, or working toward a career as a politician, taking on the role of a political leader is a big commitment that can be time-consuming, draining,

Inspiring and Cultivating the Leader in You   31

and challenging. So what drives people to do it? For most, the answer is passion. Passion is what motivates people and gives them the energy and drive to fight for what they believe in. The best political leaders are passionately committed to an issue or a cause, and they use that passion to inspire and influence others.

For some, this commitment comes naturally. Many people are born into circumstances or have life experiences that engenders an immediate connection to an issue or a cause. For example, young people who have been personally impacted by gun violence may feel especially driven to create a campaign to address gun violence in their community. LGBTQ teens who have experienced bullying because of their gender identity or sexual orientation may feel passionately driven to start a support group for other LGBTQ youth. For many others, the desire to become politically active is cultivated by awareness. Being aware of the issues that affect the people in a community, neighborhood, school, and even the world increases the likelihood that a person will be moved to get involved and take action.

Steve Jobs, a well-known introvert, was known for his innovative tech ideas and ability to motivate people to collaborate and work together.

CHAPTER THREE

THE SKILLS OF A POLITICAL LEADER

Political leadership requires many skills. All types of skills fall into two categories: hard skills and soft skills. Hard skills are abilities that can be taught and easily measured, such as typing, operating machinery, performing surgery, or programming a computer. Soft skills are essentially what we often call people skills—the skills we use to communicate and get along with

US representative Alexandria Ocasio-Cortez became the youngest congresswoman in US history by understanding the needs of her constituents.

others. Many jobs depend heavily on a person's ability to perform hard skills, but being a political leader relies heavily on soft skills. There are a number of soft skills that every aspiring political leader must master.

WRITING AND ORATORICAL SKILLS

One of the most defining moments for political leaders is when they deliver a speech. Speeches provide an opportunity for candidates to express their message in the hopes that it will not only resonate with others, but also serve as a call to action. The quality of political leaders' speeches can make or break their chances of winning the support of the public, so being a great writer and speaker is crucial for anyone aspiring to political leadership. Writing and oratorical skills are also needed to perform other duties that a political leader may be responsible for, including writing briefings or public statements, drafting legislation, speaking during meetings, creating thoughtful campaigns, and much more.

PATIENCE

Change doesn't happen overnight. Months, years, and even decades can pass before a political leader leaves her or his mark on the world. Patience allows a leader to step back and look at the bigger picture, as well as to be more open to both ideas and people. Patient leaders find it easier to listen to the concerns of others, and they are also more likely to make better decisions

Developing Political Leadership Skills

Political leaders should listen carefully to their constituents so that they understand which issues matter most to them and what they are looking for in a leader.

by considering all the options and possibilities before committing to a plan of action.

EMPATHY

Empathy is an essential leadership skill. It is the ability to understand other people's perspectives, experiences, and feelings—to put yourself in other people's shoes or see things through their eyes. It also helps leaders to communicate their ideas in ways that make sense to others and to make sense of the things people say to them. Without empathy, leaders are left without important insights about the people

INCREASE EMPATHY BY WALKING IN SOMEONE ELSE'S SHOES

Empathy is a hard skill to cultivate and scientists believe it is especially hard for teens to do so. According to a 2012 study by Ronald Dahl, a professor at the University of California Berkeley, the regions of the brain responsible for the ability to be empathetic undergo serious changes during adolescence and don't fully develop until well into adulthood, so young people struggle with the ability to be empathetic. However, just as people can lift weights to become stronger, people of any age can train their brains to become more empathetic. Practicing a technique called perceptual positions can help anyone learn to see things from someone else's point of view.

You can practice perceptual positions by following these six steps:

- Set up three chairs in a quiet, comfortable environment where you are unlikely to be interrupted.
- Close your eyes and think about a time when you disagreed with someone or got into an argument.
- Sit in the first chair and think of everything that happened during the disagreement. What did you say? What did the other person say? How did it make you feel?
- Move over to the second chair. This time, try to think about the argument from the other person's point of view. How do you think you looked to that person? How did you sound? How did that person feel?
- In the third and final chair, imagine that you are a stranger observing the argument. What are some things the stranger might suggest to the two people who are arguing to help them understand each other?
- Reflect on what you have learned and decide how you would like to move forward.

This technique can help people develop empathy by understanding what it's like to "walk in someone else's shoes."

Developing Political Leadership Skills

they are trying to reach. On the other hand, a truly empathetic leader is able to earn people's trust and support, deeply connect with others, and inspire them to take action.

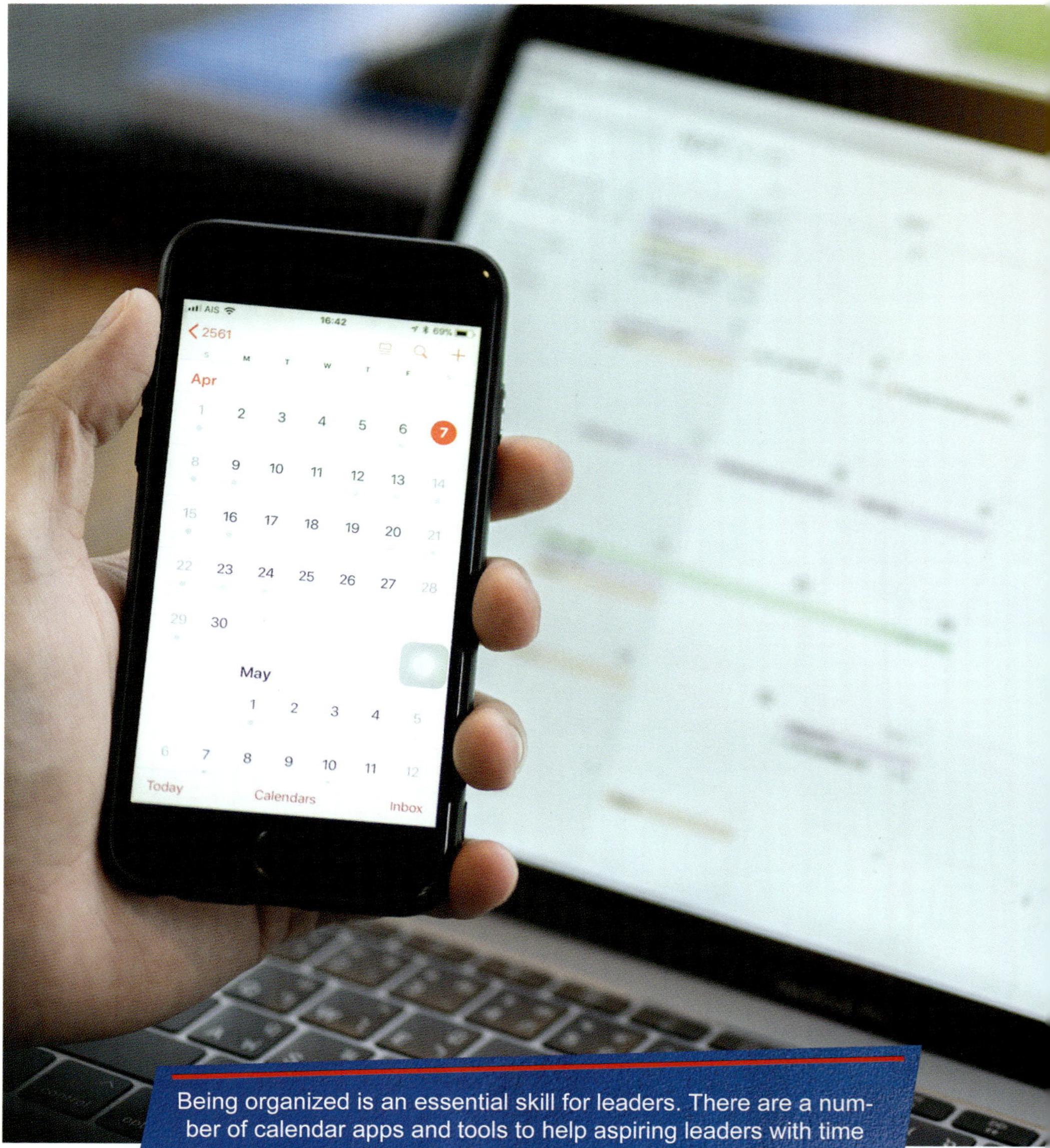

Being organized is an essential skill for leaders. There are a number of calendar apps and tools to help aspiring leaders with time management and organization.

The Skills of a Political Leader 37

TIME MANAGEMENT AND ORGANIZATIONAL SKILLS

A life in politics can quickly become busy and chaotic. There are only twenty-four hours in a day, and a political leader is expected to use every minute wisely. Organization and time management must work hand in hand to make that happen. People who properly organize their work space and schedule their days (and stick to that schedule) will not only get more done, but also do those things more effectively.

PROBLEM SOLVING AND CONFLICT RESOLUTION

Solving problems and resolving conflicts are the very essence of what a political leader does. When anything goes wrong, people look to leaders for answers and a plan of action. It is also common for political leaders to gain support and win votes by promising to address long-standing issues. To make good on a promise like that, leaders must flex their problem-solving skills by coming up with great solutions and implementing them. Political leaders are usually judged by the effectiveness of their solutions. More effective leaders have longer careers.

TEAMWORK AND WORK ETHIC

Hard work and collaboration form the cornerstone of a successful political career. To run a campaign or implement new ideas, a leader must work with a team of people and that group of people must all be committed and motivated. A team or group works best when there is a hardworking leader to serve as a role model. Leaders who are not dedicated and hardworking cannot expect their team to be those things either.

Many young people are a driving force behind national political campaigns. Working a phone bank for a political candidate is a great way to help out and gain skills.

RESEARCH SKILLS

Research skills are needed for many aspects of political leadership. Whether a person is developing a campaign strategy or writing a well-informed speech, thorough research provides insight and strengthens the arguments and claims being made. There are many ways to conduct research. While Google is a great tool for getting access to lots of information very quickly, it is not the only way (and sometimes not the most effective way) to do research. Great researchers conduct interviews, scour libraries for informative books, magazines, and documents, and ask experts who are knowledgeable in the subject area.

UNDERSTAND SOCIAL MEDIA AND TECHNOLOGY

Social media is an important tool that can be used to amplify political messages, reach a target audience, and connect with potential allies. Political candidates who want to be competitive in today's social media–driven world must know how to use all kinds of different social media platforms. They should also be skilled at coming up with novel, interesting ways to use those platforms. Being a successful leader means staying ahead of the curve when it comes to technology and finding new ways of connecting with potential voters.

TIPS FOR WRITING AND DELIVERING POWERFUL SPEECHES

Speeches provide an opportunity for candidates to express their message in the hopes that it will not only resonate with others, but also serve as a call to action. The quality of a speech can make or break a candidate's chance of winning the support of the public. The following are a few tricks and tips to help make sure a speech is in top shape and powerfully delivered.

To be the best, learn from the best. Read and watch inspiring speeches by other people and analyze what makes the speech work. Exposure to great writing and delivery provides invaluable lessons that can boost your writing, oratorical skills, and self-esteem.

Research and understand your audience. How old is your audience? What issues are important to them? When you truly understand your audience, you are more likely to know how to connect with them.

Be clear and concise. A short and to-the-point speech is best. Minimize the use of long sentences or unnecessary words that could be confusing or distract from the message you are trying to convey.

Be a storyteller. While facts are important, a speech with too many facts can quickly become boring. Try to weave facts and your message into an engaging story. People will be more likely to listen and engage when the speech has a compelling narrative.

Speak with authority. Political leaders are expected to be confident and exhibit certainty. Deliver every statement with confidence.

Revise and practice (over and over again). After you write your first draft, read it aloud to yourself or to friends or family. Reading it aloud will help you practice your delivery as well as catch unnecessary words.

Play with sound. Your voice is an instrument that is capable of many pitches and rhythms. Great speakers pay close attention to intonation and play with the rhythm and volume of different words and sentences.

MAKE CONNECTIONS AND BUILD NETWORKS

Connecting with others and networking is undoubtedly one of the most important skills that political leaders must master. Leaders are only as strong as their network. Those who are well connected can draw supporters from all over a school, town, state, or even country. To connect with other people and win their support, political leaders must show that they genuinely care and want to work in the best interest of their constituents. They must also maintain those connections over time by staying in touch and being generous with their time and resources.

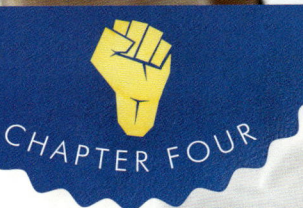

CHAPTER FOUR

GET TRAINED, GET INVOLVED!

Young people have the right to be involved in the big decisions that will impact their lives, and the only way to exercise that right is by becoming politically engaged. However, political engagement is not always easy for young people. Many older people assume that young people are not worthy of positions in political leadership. This is a major barrier that is only reinforced when youth do not engage in the political process or develop their leadership skills. Luckily, there are many ways young people can prepare themselves for political leadership with both formal and informal training.

WHERE TO GET FORMALLY TRAINED

There are many organizations created to support young people who are interested in becoming political leaders. Some provide formal leadership training or offer ways for young people to connect with leaders

Get Trained, Get Involved!

Young people can gain leadership experience by taking part in mock elections. By playing the roles of elected officials and candidates, they obtain valuable skills.

in their communities and beyond. Others provide opportunities for young people to learn more about the political process by participating in mock elections and attending workshops on all aspects of government.

THE NATIONAL STUDENT LEADERSHIP FOUNDATION

The National Student Leadership Foundation (NSLF) is a nonprofit organization established in 1989 that offers political leadership training programs for middle and high schoolers over the summer, called the National Student Leadership Conference (NSLC). Students who participate in these programs get to experience life on a college campus, build and develop their political leadership skills, and also meet with leaders from all across the nation! Participation in NSLF programs also prepares young people for college and careers in fields including business, science, politics, and more. There is a tuition fee, but there are also many scholarship opportunities to offset the cost for those who may not be able to afford it. Students can find out more about NSLF and the NSLC at www.nslcleaders.org.

BOYS STATE AND GIRLS STATE

Every year, high schools across the country choose one or two juniors or seniors to participate in Boys State and Girl State—two separate programs sponsored by The American Legion and The American Legion Auxiliary that bring the most politically talented students together to create a mock version of the US government. These summer programs offer the opportunity for participants to take part in a number of mock political scenarios, including running for office, electing officials, drafting and debating bills, and making motions. Some programs offer city and county mock courts and a state supreme court, with the participants acting as lawyers, judges, plaintiffs, defendants, and jury members. There are also lectures and workshops to help students become experts in all aspects of government and politics. This experience is fully immersive and offers hands-on experience that not only helps participants learn the ins and outs of US government and politics but also helps build confidence. Youth interested in finding out more information about Boys State and Girls State can contact their local American Legion (www.legion.org) or The American Legion Auxiliary (www.alaforveterans.org).

YMCA YOUTH AND GOVERNMENT

The YMCA Youth and Government is a national program that brings young people from all across the world together to literally practice democracy by participating in mock government. This program operates in local YMCAs throughout the year and culminates in a statewide conference where representatives from local Ys act like delegates, with youth getting together to debate issues affecting their mock state and suggest legislation. Students can find more information about these programs at www.ymca.net/youthandgovernment.

OTHER WAYS TO DEVELOP POLITICAL LEADERSHIP SKILLS

Developing political leadership skills is a lifelong process. While it is beneficial to have formal training and experience as a political leader, there are many other ways to develop the crucial skills political leaders need. In addition to formal training, young people can learn by joining school clubs, volunteering on political campaigns, helping to organize political fundraisers,

Many schools hold student elections. These events provide an opportunity for aspiring leaders to work on their people skills and learn how to win the support of their peers.

attending local council meetings, joining a school or community board, and getting involved in activist organizations around issues they care about.

PARTICIPATE IN STUDENT GOVERNMENT

Just about every school has a student government and needs students to play several roles, including president, vice president, secretary, and treasurer.

HOW TO START A CLUB

Some students are lucky enough to attend schools where there is an abundance of clubs to join and activities to participate in. For others, their first step toward developing political leadership skills may well be addressing the fact that their school has limited options—and doing something about it. Students who are interested in establishing a club at their school can follow a few important steps to obtain the support and funding needed to get started:

- Figure out the purpose of the club
- Find other students who are interested in joining
- Reach out to school faculty to get permission to start the club and find a chaperone
- Raise money to get the club started
- If the club exists on a national level (for example, Key Club), contact the club's state or national headquarters to get support and resources for your club.

Students who are appointed or elected to their school's student government are typically in charge of managing all of the activities, programs, and initiatives surrounding their school. This opportunity offers a crash course in building political leadership skills. From creating and promoting a campaign to time management and delivering speeches, participants in student government learn important skills that will serve them in any career, but especially in political leadership positions.

JOIN KEY CLUB

Key Club is a student-led club that promotes leadership and focuses on giving back to the community. Members of this club typically do acts of community service, such as cleaning up parks and organizing food or clothing drives. By dedicating themselves to helping their community, Key Club members learn to be proactive about solving problems and how to affect change in their community. Participation in the club also builds confidence and character.

JOIN DEBATE CLUB

Debate club is a fun way for students to learn how to express their beliefs clearly and concisely. Members are expected to craft and deliver solid arguments and compete with students from other schools. Those who write and deliver the best speeches are often invited to competitions in their state. Debate club allows students to hone their writing and oratorical skills in a competitive but safe environment.

Organizations such as debate clubs can be a fun way for young people to hone their public speaking skills and work on their persuasion techniques.

PLAY TEAM SPORTS

There is no "I" in team and there's no easier way to learn the importance of teamwork than by playing a team sport. A great sports team is made up of players who are not only athletic, but also strong communicators who are committed to training and being respectful of one another. Through participating in a team sport, aspiring leaders can learn many crucial skills, including time management, commitment, communication, and how to connect with peers to build a strong, unified team.

TUTOR YOUR PEERS

Sometimes a student needs help learning a difficult concept or mastering an academic skill, and schools often look to other students to help out. Peer tutoring serves two purposes: it gives struggling students the support they need, and it also gives the tutoring students a chance to take on the role of an educator. Peer tutors get to hone their communication and empathy skills while giving back to their schools. They build stronger relationships with other students by taking an interest and investing in their achievement.

GET AN AFTER-SCHOOL JOB

A lot of planning and preparation goes into finding and securing a job, even an after-school job. Job seekers must not only find companies interested in hiring, they

50 Developing Political Leadership Skills

must also make themselves hirable by crafting strong résumés and doing well in interviews. These are very daunting tasks for many people. Searching for an after-school job will help you hone many key leadership skills. Working that job will also help you develop crucial skills, such as punctuality, conscientiousness, and people skills.

VOLUNTEER FOR A POLITICAL CAMPAIGN

Just as every vote counts in an election, so does every volunteer. Volunteers are crucial in political campaigns. They help to register and mobilize voters, and they

People of any age can volunteer to help with canvassing for a local political campaign. This means going door-to-door in the community to drop brochures and speak with voters.

educate the community about the candidates and their positions. Many campaigns welcome students who are eager to lend a helping hand. Working for a campaign is a surefire way to make a positive change, and it can serve as a great learning opportunity for young people. It is generally a very flexible commitment that can be worked into any schedule. For those interested in volunteering for a presidential campaign, looking on a candidate's website for opportunities is a great place to start. Volunteers are also needed for local elections. Pay a visit to the offices of your local candidates and offer to help out—this work is just as important as working on national campaigns!

JOIN AN ACTIVIST ORGANIZATION

There are many activist organizations that value the engagement of young people. Some even have divisions specifically for youth. Girl Scouts/Boy Scouts, the Global Youth Action Network, Taking It Global, NAACP Youth and College Division, the National Youth and Student Peace Coalition, Feminist Campus, and Global Youth Alliance are just some of the many organizations that welcome young people, groom them for political leadership, and get them active in their communities—and the world.

THE FUTURE IS YOURS

Young people can be informed, passionate, driven, and engaged political leaders with the power to influence and change the world. The first step toward

52 Developing Political Leadership Skills

There are so many ways for young people to come together, speak up, and make their voices heard in the political arena.

that is developing political leadership skills. Whether you aspire to take on a political role in your school or local community or you want to become president or a senator one day, you will need many of the same political leadership skills to get there. It is never too early to hone those skills and practice using them. For young people who want to leave their mark, the time to start is now!

GLOSSARY

budgeting Coming up with a plan for how money should be spent.
conflict resolution A skill used to find fair solutions to disputes between people.
conscientiousness A personality trait that describes the natural tendency to work hard and be dutiful.
constituency A body of voters who elect political leaders in a specific district.
empathy The ability to understand and view things from someone else's perspective.
extroversion A personality trait that describes people who are outwardly focused and less interested in their internal thoughts.
introversion A personality trait that describes people who focus more on their internal thoughts than things happening externally.
jurisdiction An area where a political leader has influence and power, for example, a school, town, city, or state.
network A connected group of people who provide support for each other.
neuroticism A personality trait that describes the natural tendency to experience negative emotions, like anxiety, worry, fear, anger, or jealousy.
passion A strong feeling that drives individuals to act, say something, or do something about a political issue.
perceptual positions An empathy-building technique in which the participant practices viewing a situation from different points of view.

political activist A person who seeks to make political change or raise awareness about a specific issue.
political campaign An organized effort to influence the outcome of an election.
political candidate A person nominated to run for political office in local, state, or national elections.
school board A group of elected leaders responsible for the maintenance of a school and its budgeting.
soft skills Also known as people skills; skills used to build and maintain relationships.
status quo The established way of doing things, especially in politics.
work ethic The quality of working hard and being responsible.

FOR MORE INFORMATION

American Council of Young Political Leaders (ACYPL)
1030 15th Street NW, Suite 580 West
Washington, DC 20005
(202) 857-0999
Website: https://www.acypl.org
Facebook: @ACYPL
The ACYPL is an internationally recognized organization that introduces young political leaders to global politics through international exchange programs.

American Legion National Headquarters
700 N. Pennsylvania Street
PO Box 1055
Indianapolis, IN 46206
(317) 630-1200
Website: https://www.legion.org
Facebook: @AmericanLegionHQ
Instagram: @TheAmericanLegion
Twitter: @AmericanLegion
The American Legion is a veteran's organization dedicated to mentoring youth through various programs.

Canada World Youth
2330 Notre-Dame Street West, Suite 300
Montreal, QC, H3J 1N4
Canada
(514) 931-3526 or (1-800) 605-3526
Website: http://canadaworldyouth.org

Facebook: @CanadaWorldYouth
.JeunesseCanadaMonde
Twitter: @CWYJCM
Canada World Youth is an organization that helps Canadian young people develop political leadership skills and work to make change through volunteer opportunities both at home and abroad.

National Democratic Institute
455 Massachusetts Avenue NW, 8th Floor
Washington, DC 20001-2621
(202) 728-5500
Website: https://www.ndi.org
Facebook: @National.Democratic.Institute
Twitter: @NDI
The National Democratic Institute works to increase political engagement in countries all over the world.

YMCA of the USA
101 North Wacker Drive
Chicago, IL 60606
1-(800) 872-9622
Website: https://www.ymca.net
Facebook: @ymcanyc
Twitter: @ymca
The YMCA is a community-focused organization with various programs to help young people develop leadership skills.

Young Diplomats of Canada
Website: http://youngdiplomats.ca
Facebook, Instagram, and Twitter: @YDCanada

For More Information

Young Diplomats of Canada offers hands-on training to youth to help them establish leadership and international advocacy experience.

Youth Service America (YSA)
1050 Connecticut Avenue NW, Room 65525
Washington, DC 20035
(202) 296-2992
Website: https://ysa.org
Facebook: @YouthServiceAmerica
Twitter: @YouthService
The YSA is an organization that works to increase youth community engagement through volunteer opportunities.

FOR FURTHER READING

Bishop, Sue. *Develop Your Assertiveness*. London, UK: Kogan Page, 2013.

Cialdini, Robert B. *Influence: The Psychology of Persuasion*. New York, NY: Harper Collins Publishers, 2016.

Covey, Stephen R. *The 7 Habits of Highly Effective People: Powerful Lessons in Personal Change*. New York, NY: Free Press, 2014.

Freedman, Jeri. *Being a Leader: Organizing and Inspiring a Group*. New York, NY: Rosen Publishing, 2012.

Harper, Leslie. *How to Raise Money for a Cause*. New York, NY: PowerKids Press, 2015.

Lanik, Martin. *The Leader Habit: Master the Skills You Need to Lead—In Just Minutes a Day*. New York, NY: American Management Association, 2018.

Parr, Ben. *Captivology: The Science of Capturing People's Attention*. New York, NY: HarperOne, 2015.

Tebow, Tim. *Shaken: Fighting to Stand Strong No Matter What Comes Your Way*. Colorado Springs, CO: WaterBrook, 2017.

Weatherford, Carole Boston, and Robert Barrett. *Obama: Only in America*. Las Vegas, NV: Two Lions, 2014.

Yousafzai, Malala, and Patricia McCormick. *I Am Malala: How One Girl Stood up for Education and Changed the World*. New York, NY: Little, Brown and Company, 2016.

BIBLIOGRAPHY

Baker, Peter. "Education of a President." *New York Times Magazine*, October 12, 2010. https://www.nytimes.com/2010/10/17/magazine/17obama-t.html.

Cain, Susan. "Must Great Leaders Be Gregarious?" *New York Times*, September 15, 2012. https://www.nytimes.com/2012/09/16/opinion/sunday/introverts-make-great-leaders-too.html.

Center for Creative Leadership. "The Core Leadership Skills You Need in Every Role." Retrieved March 13, 2019. https://www.ccl.org/articles/leading-effectively-articles/fundamental-4-core-leadership-skills-for-every-career-stage.

Covey, Stephen. *The 7 Habits of Highly Effective People: Restoring the Character Ethic*. New York, NY: Free Press, 2004.

Ferguson Publishing. *Leadership Skills*. New York, NY: Ferguson, 2009.

Fortin, Jacey. "'Access to Literacy' Is Not a Constitutional Right, Judge in Detroit Rules." *New York Times*, July 4, 2018. https://www.nytimes.com/2018/07/04/education/detroit-public-schools-education.html.

Freedman, Jeri. *Being a Leader: Organizing and Inspiring a Group*. New York, NY: Rosen Publishing, 2012.

Gilson, Dave. "Presidents Kissing Babies: A Short History." *Mother Jones*, January 17, 2012. https://www.motherjones.com/media/2012/01/politicians-kissing-babies-brief-history.

International Institute for Management Development. "25 Leadership Skills You Need to Learn Fast."

Retrieved March 13, 2019. https://www.imd.org/imd-reflections/leadership-reflections/leadership-skills.

Kriss, Brady. "What's Tech Got to Do with Political Activism? Everything." Recode, April 17, 2018. https://www.recode.net/2018/4/17/17243808/silicon-valley-politics-activism-volunteer-march-for-our-lives-ragtag.

Lanik, Martin. *The Leader Habit: Master the Skills You Need to Lead—In Just Minutes a Day*. New York, NY: American Management Association, 2018.

National Democratic Institute. "DemTools." Retrieved March 13, 2019. https://www.ndi.org/demtools.

NLP Techniques. "Perceptual Positions." Retrieved March 13, 2019. https://www.nlp-techniques.org/what-is-nlp/perceptual-positions.

Rampton, John. "10 U.S. Presidents Who Were Introverts." Inc., August 21, 2015. https://www.inc.com/john-rampton/are-you-an-introvert-so-were-these-10-us-presidents.html.

Samuels, Alex. "Mike Floyd's First Job After Graduating High School? Helping Run a School District." *Texas Tribune*, May 26, 2017. https://www.texastribune.org/2017/05/26/meet-mike-floyd-18-year-old-elected-pearlands-school-board.

Sit, Ryan. "More Than 2 Million in 90 Percent of Voting Districts Joined March for Our Lives Protests." *Newsweek*, March 26, 2018. https://www.newsweek.com/march-our-lives-how-many-2-million-90-voting-district-860841.

INDEX

A
anxiety, 24, 26–28

B
Black Lives Matter movement, 16
Boys State, 44–45
breathing, deep, 26, 27
budgeting, 8
Burke, Tarana, 16, 18

C
Cancel, Sixto, 18
city council, 8, 10
   members of, 8
conflict resolution, 37
Congress, 10, 11
conscientiousness, 21, 28, 50
   tips for increasing, 29–30
constituents, 12, 41
   base of, 10

D
debate club, 48
debates, 14
distractions, 30, 40
   from anxious thoughts, 27

E
elected officials, 7
   definition of, 8–10
   empathy, 22–23, 25, 34, 35, 36
   skills, 49
extroversion, 21
   contrasted with introversion, 22–23
extroverts, 22, 23–24
   leaders, 20

F
Floyd, Mike, 11

G
Gary B. v. Snyder, 29
Girls State, 44–45
Global Youth Action Network, 51

H
hard skills, 32, 33, 35
House of Representatives, 10

I
introversion, 21, 25
   contrasted with extroversion, 22–23
introverts, 22–23
   as leaders, 23–24
   presidents, 25

J
Jackson, Andrew, 11–12
Jennings, Jazz, 16
job, after-school, 49–50
jurisdiction, 8

K

Kasky, Cameron, 15
Key Club, 47, 48
King, Martin Luther Jr., 16

L

Lincoln, Abraham, 4, 25

M

March for Our Lives, 15
Marjory Stoneman Douglas
 High School, 15
mayors, 8–9
meditation, 26, 27

N

National Student Leadership
 Conference (NSLC), 43–44
National Student Leadership
 Foundation (NSLF), 43–44
networks
 building, 41
 student, 11
neuroticism, 21, 24, 26
Nobel Peace Prize, 16

O

Obama, Barack, 4, 25
oratorical skills, 25, 33, 40, 48
organizational skills, 28, 37

P

Parks, Rosa, 16
passion, 6, 19, 20, 30–31, 51
patience, 6, 33–34
peer tutoring, 49
perceptual positions, 35
personality, 20
 and leadership, 21
 traits, 21, 23, 24
 types, 20
plans
 of action, 33–34, 37
 for a demonstration, 15
 following through on, 28, 30
 to get a job, 49
 having, 28
 importance of, 30
political activists, 7, 14–16, 18
 organizations, 45–46, 51
political campaigns, 45–46
 volunteering for, 50–51
political candidates, 11, 12,
 14, 39
 in debates and forums, 14
 lives of, 10
 public image of, 11, 12
presidents, 4, 6, 9–10, 12, 25
 Abraham Lincoln, 4, 25
 Andrew Jackson, 11–12
 Barack Obama, 4, 25
 becoming, 6, 52
 campaign, 51
 impeachment of, 10
 introverted, 25
 John F. Kennedy, 25

Index

Richard Nixon, 25
Thomas Jefferson, 25
problem solving, 37
public image, 11–13

R

Ragtag, 15
Rao, Gitanjali, 18
research skills, 39

S

school board, 10, 11
   members of, 8–9, 11
self-confidence, 26–28
senators, 4, 10, 52
slavery, 4
Smart Wildfire Sensor, 19
social media, 16, 18, 24
   understanding, 39
soft skills, 32–33
speeches, 14–15, 16, 25, 26, 33, 39, 47, 48
   tips for powerful, 25, 40
sports, 49
status quo, 16
Steinem, Gloria, 16
student government, 6, 30, 46–47

T

teamwork, 38, 49
technology
   and activism, 15, 16, 18–19
   understanding, 39

time management, 37, 47, 49
Truth, Sojourner, 4

V

volunteers, 15, 45–46, 50–51

W

work ethic, 38
writing, 33, 48
   speech, 39
   tips for, 40

Y

YMCA Youth and Government, 45
Yousafzai, Malala, 14

ABOUT THE AUTHOR

Tiffanie Drayton is a writer from Jersey City, New Jersey, who has worked closely with prominent political leaders. Her work advocating for social justice has been featured in many publications and is often used in university curricula. You can reach out to her on Twitter @draytontiffanie.

PHOTO CREDITS

Cover Jamie Grill/The Image Bank/Getty Images; pp. 4–5 (background graphics) weerawan/iStock/Getty Images; p. 5 Library of Congress Prints and Photographs; p. 7 (inset) SOPA Images/LightRocket/Getty Images; pp. 8–9 Brendan Smialowski/AFP/Getty Images; pp. 12–13 Official White House Photo by Pete Souza; p. 17 AFP/Getty Images; p. 21 GaudiLab/Shutterstock.com; p. 23 Johner Images/Getty Images; p. 25 Photo12/UIG/Getty Images; p. 27 fizkes/Shutterstock.com; p. 31 Sean Gallup/Getty Images; p. 32 (inset) Alex Wong/Getty Images; p. 34 The Washington Post/Getty Images; pp. 36–37 Kanut Srinin/Shutterstock.com; p. 38 Barbara Davidson/Getty Images; p. 43 Jeffrey Greenberg/UIG/Getty Images; p. 46 Image Source/Photodisc/Getty Images; p. 48 Monkey Business Images/Shutterstock.com; p. 50 John Leyba/The Denver Post/Getty Images; p. 52 NurPhoto/Getty Images; additional graphic elements moodboard - Mike Watson Images/Brand X Pictures/Getty Images (chapter opener backgrounds), Maksim M/Shutterstock.com (fists).

Design and Layout: Michael Moy; Editor: Rachel Aimee; Photo Researcher: Nicole DiMella